this food thing

ROSALIA BARRESI

AuthorHouse™ UK
1663 Liberty Drive
Bloomington, IN 47403 USA
www.authorhouse.co.uk
Phone: 0800 047 8203 (Domestic TFN)
+44 1908 723714 (International)

Published by AuthorHouse 06/11/2019

ISBN: 978-1-7283-8877-9 (sc)
ISBN: 978-1-7283-8878-6 (e)

authorHOUSE®

My name is **Rosalia Barresi** and I am a complementary therapist and nutritionist working in and around Oxfordshire, Buckinghamshire, Berkshire and London.

My love of food has evolved over the years, coming from a Sicilian family, I learnt from an early age the benefits of quality fresh seasonal produce being turned into great cuisine.

Over some years, I have been fortunate to learn in many foodie environments including front of house management in a north London vegetarian restaurant called Manna. This has evolved into a Vegan establishment I highly recommend. I love cooking, especially for and around others, sharing the Kitchen is a great social experiment, which can be an awesome focal point for family and friends.

My own experiences were always of family and particularly my own Mum, a true Matriarch, who from an early age drew us into the magic she created in the kitchen. I was also fortunate to run a community cafe for five years for a mental health charity in Oxfordshire. A community project out of Thame, where locals enjoyed inexpensive, delicious, healthy meals based around fresh local seasonal produce.

Although not vegetarian, my roles in Nutrition and Health have driven me to create meals that are not only healthy but tasty and easy to prepare. The vegetarian aspect is environmental too.

As a therapist, I realised that by eating healthier options, this, in turn, improves our health and well being.. a no-brainer! The benefits of preventative medicine are never better displayed than with the right nutrients and vitamins we can absorb through eating fresh, healthy, seasonal produce.

Food can truly be a medicine, it's not rocket science.

These recipes, forged through my experiences in Food, Nutrition and Family are my way of helping create better options for today's busy lifestyle.

Buon Appetito

Twitter / Instagram

@rosbarresi

breakfast
· · · · · · · · · · · · · · · · · · ·

- b r e a k f a s t -

ALMOND CEREAL

4 S E R V I N G S

 20"   NUTS   FRUITS   OVEN   140°C

INGREDIENTS.

3 tbsp coconut oil melted

150 grams flaked almonds

2 tbsp chia or flax seeds

3 tbsp raw nuts of your choice

2 tbsp rice syrup (optional)

RECIPE.

Preheat the oven to 140 degrees or gas mark 4/5.

Place all the ingredients onto a baking sheet and pour over the oil and syrup and mix well.

Bake for about 15 minutes.

Leave to cool and transfer to container.

Serve with fruit and yoghurt.

Very Healthy for the Morning

CARROT SOUP WITH KALE & CHILLI SALSA

2 SERVINGS

 35" VEGGIES POT

INGREDIENTS.

For the soup

5 large carrots, peeled and chopped

2 cloves garlic peeled

1 large onion peeled and chopped

1 tbsp Bouillon stock

1 tbsp butter

1 pint water

Seasoning

1 tbsp honey

For the salsa

3 Kale leaves

1 red chilli

Juice half lemon

20 grams rocket leaves

2 tbsp rapeseed oil

RECIPE.

Place the butter in a large saucepan and melt, add the onion, garlic and carrots and stir for about 2 mins.

Season and add the stock, seasoning and stir well.

Add the water and leave to bring to the boil on gentle heat.

Taste and season if needed. Add the honey and simmer for about 30 minutes.

When cooked leave to cool for sometime and the blitz until smooth.

For the salsa, place all the ingredients in a food processor and blitz until it becomes well mixed and resembles a salsa.

Serve with the soup to add taste and texture…

ROASTED PEPPER WITH MOZZARELLA & BROCCOLI PESTO

2 SERVINGS

 15" BALANCE VEGGIES

INGREDIENTS.

One yellow pepper

Broccoli pesto; 10 grams rocket, 70 grams broccoli, juice of one lemon, seasoning and olive oil.

150 grams mozzarella

60 grams mushrooms

1 avocado

Seasoning

5 cdf. Bibendum

RECIPE.

To make the pesto blitz the ingredients in a food processor.

Preheat the oven to 160 degrees.

Cut the pepper in two and place on a baking tray, drizzle olive oil on it and season and place in oven for about ten minutes.

Meanwhile fry the mushrooms and mash the avocado and place on a plate. Drizzle olive oil and season.

Remove the pepper from oven and stuff with mozzarella and pesto. Place back in oven for about ten more minutes.

When mushrooms are cooked place on top of avocado.

When pepper is cooked serve on the avocado and mushrooms.

Enjoy!!.

veggies

BROAD BEAN, CHILLI & RICOTTA FILLED ROASTED RED PEPPERS

2 SERVINGS

 40" BALANCE VEGGIES

INGREDIENTS.

2 Long red peppers

150g Broad Beans - fresh or frozen

A glut of r apeseed oil

Seasoning

2 Sticks of celery

1 Green chilli

10 Grams parsley

Juice half lemon

1 tsp Bouillon stock

200 grams Ricotta cheese

RECIPE.

Preheat oven to 160 degrees, and then cut the peppers down one side, lay on baking sheet, drizzle some oil on and season. Place in the oven.

Meanwhile peel and shell the beans and cook on moderate heat for until cooked.

When cooked blend in food processor with all the other ingredients adding the Ricotta at the end. Make sure it is well seasoned and add more if needed.

When the peppers have been cooking for about 20 minutes take out of oven, fill each pepper with the broad bean mixture once it had been blitzed.

Cook for further 15 minutes and grill for five minutes. Serve alone or with chicken, salad or serve as a pasta sauce.

veggies

BROAD BEAN & CREAM CHEESE WITH PASTA

2 SERVINGS

 25"   BALANCE   VEGGIES

INGREDIENTS.

200 grams pasta

150 grams broad beans

Butter for cooking

1 small red onion

3 cloves garlic

1 tsp Bouillon stock

2 tbsp red wine

Seasoning

50 grams cream cheese

30 grams parmesan

RECIPE.

Fry the onion and garlic in some butter and season well.

Add the stock, the broad beans and wine. Stir well.

Cook on low heat and leave for fifteen minutes.

In the meantime heat some water for the pasta.

Add the cream cheese to the broad bean mixture and stir in well.

When the pasta is cooked add this to the mixture and mix well.

Grate the parmesan on the top and serve!

Yummy….

ROASTED BUTTERNUT SQUASH, SWEET POTATO & HALLOUMI, WITH BROAD BEAN, CABBAGE & AVOCADO CREAM

2 SERVINGS

 15"   BALANCE   VEGGIES

INGREDIENTS.

Half butternut squash peeled, sliced and cubed

1 small sweet potato, peeled and cubed

3 to 4 chestnut mushrooms, sliced

225 grams halloumi cheese cubed

150 grams broad beans cooked

Juice half lemon

1 half avocado

50 grams cooked green cabbage

Seasoning

1 small red onion chopped

3 cloves garlic sliced

1 tsp Bouillon stock

Few tbsp olive oil for roasting and for cream

Few basil leaves

RECIPE.

Preheat oven to 160 degrees. Place the squash and sweet potato onto a baking tray and season and pour over the olive oil. Roast for about twenty minutes. In a sauce pan fry the onion, garlic and add the stock and season. Leave to one side. Take out the squash from the oven and add the mushrooms and halloumi. Bake for a further fifteen to twenty minutes.

In a food processor, add the lemon juice, avocado, seasoning, cabbage and the basil leaves as well as olive oil, add the cooked onion and garlic. Blitz until creamy. Leave to one side.

Remove the squash etc from the oven and place onto a serving dish, Scatter the cooked broad beans and then spoon the creamy avocado mixture on the top. Pour a little olive oil on the top and season. Serve!

BUTTERNUT SQUASH, FLAGOLET BEAN AND MUSHROOM LASAGNE

2 SERVINGS

 15" BALANCE VEGGIES

INGREDIENTS.

Half buttersquash thinl y sliced

100 grams sliced mushrooms

265 grams flageolet beans

400 grams tomato passata

4 cloves garlic peeled/sliced

1 small red onion sliced

10 grams fresh chopped basil

150 grams cream cheese

1 tsp Bouillon stock

seasoning

1 tbsp paprika

100 grams frozen peas.

RECIPE.

Preheat the oven to 160 degrees. Lay the butternut squash on a baking sheet and drizzle oil and season. Cook for around 20 minutes. Meanwhile, in a pan heat up some butter and cook the garlic and onion. Season, add the stock and beans. Stir well, add the passata and cook for about ten minutes on a medium heat. Season again if needed. Add the peas. Remove the squash from the oven, and take the passata off the heat. Take an oven proof dish around 8 inches in diameter all around.

Pour a layer of sauce on the base of the dish and lay some sheets of the squash on top. Spread the cream cheese on the squash and layer some mushrooms. Keep doing this until the ingredients have all been used ending with some sauce so it does not dry in the oven. Bake in the oven for about 35 minutes.

Serve with plenty of greens!

veggies

CAULIFLOWER PIZZA

2 SERVINGS

 15"   BALANCE   VEGGIES

INGREDIENTS.

For the base:

250 grams cauliflower (blitzed up)

100 grams ground almonds

1 egg beaten

Seasoning

2 tbsp rape seed oil

For the topping;

3 large mushrooms

75 grams soft goats cheese

20 grams rocket leaves

Cherry tomatoes

2 tbsp olive oil

Seasoning

RECIPE.

Preheat the oven to about 160 degrees. Place the cauliflower in a large mixing bowl, add the almonds, seasoning and egg and mix well. Lay in four small sections on greaseproof paper, on a baking sheet and place in the oven.

Cook for about 20 minutes and then turn over and cook on other side for about 5 mins.

Remove from oven and put the mushrooms, tomatoes and olive oil on the base. Season well and place in the oven for five mins.

Remove and then add the goats cheese and put back in the oven. Cook for further 10 minutes. Take out and place the rocket leaves on the top and enjoy!!

Yummy!

BROCCOLI PESTO PASTA WITH MOZZARELLA

2 SERVINGS

 20" BALANCE VEGGIES

INGREDIENTS.

For the pesto:

10 grams rocket

juice of one lemon

1 tbsp olive oil

seasoning

70 grams broccoli

Plus;

100 grams broad beans

70 grams gluten free pasta

Buffalo mozzarella

RECIPE

Cook the broad beans in a pan for about ten minutes, meanwhile in a food processor blitz the rocket, lemon juice, olive oil, broccoli and seasoning.

Blitz until smooth. Leave to one side. Cook pasta in water and when ready incorporate with the broad beans.

Chop up the mozzarella and add to pasta and beans. In a pan mix it all up with the pesto mix, season again if needed and serve.

Yummy!

v e g g i e s

HALLOUMI, MUSHROOM & BEETROOT SALAD

2 SERVINGS

 15" BALANCE VEGGIES

INGREDIENTS.

100 grams halloumi (sliced)

3 small pickled beetroot (sliced)

1 small onion, 1 clove garlic (both chopped)

100 grams chopped button mushrooms

handful rocket

seasoning

For the dressing

2 tbsp tahini

juice half lemon

1 tbsp cider vinegar

1 tbsp olive oil

RECIPE.

Fry the onions and garlic in some butter for a few minutes, season well.

Add the mushrooms and fry for few minutes more.

Arrange the rocket and beetroot on a plate, layer the mushrooms on top when cooked.

In the same pan add the Halloumi and fry on each side for a couple minutes.

Place on top of the mushrooms. For the dressing mix all the ingredients well in a bowl, season and pour over the salad.

Enjoy!!!

VEGETABLE HUMMUS WITH ROASTED VEGETABLES

2 SERVINGS

 40" BALANCE VEGGIES

INGREDIENTS.

1 Sweet potato peeled & chopped

1 small red onion chopped

4 cloves garlic

1 courgette chopped

1 leek chopped

Rapeseed oil

Juice half lemon

1 tbsp tahini

Seasoning

RECIPE.

Preheat oven to 180 degrees. Prepare the veg and roast for 30 mins.

When roasted place some of it in a food processor with the tahini, lemon juice, seasoning and oil.

Blitz until well mixed and serve with the remaining veg or use as a dip!

GOAT CHEESE TART

2 SERVINGS

 15" BALANCE VEGGIES

INGREDIENTS.

the pastry

180 grams ground almonds

2 tbsp coconut oil

2 medium eggs

extra oil for greasing

for the filling

120 grams soft goats cheese

1 egg beaten

10 grams chopped chives

1 large medium heat chilli chopped

1 tsp paprika

Seasoning

RECIPE.

Melt the coconut oil in a pan and leave to cool. Place the almonds into a pan, add the oil and stir well. Add the eggs and mix until it binds together. Scoop it all up and cling film it. Leave in fridge for an hour or two until it firm ups.

Preheat the oven to about 180 degrees.

Place the goat cheese, chives, chilli and paprika in a bowl and mix well. Combine well and place in fridge for about twenty minutes.

Remove pastry from the fridge and roll out to about half centimetre thick. The pastry can be quite sticky so it is good to roll it under the cling film.

Use a cookie cutter to cut out eight to ten rounds.

Grease a muffin tin and using a pallet knife place each round into the muffin tin. Blind bake for about fifteen minutes. No cooking beads needed. Remove from oven and evenly spoon the mixture into each tart case. Place back in oven for about twenty minutes. The tops should to slightly golden.

Remove from oven and serve with salad. Yum!!

veggies

COURGETTI, SWEET POTATO & HALLOUMI CRUMBLE

2 SERVINGS

 15" BALANCE VEGGIES

INGREDIENTS.

large courgette spiralised

1 sweet potato peeled & chopped

1 small onion finely chopped

4 cloves garlic finely chopped

Seasoning

2 spring onions

1 tsp Boullion Stock

1 tsp fennel seeds

250 grams halloumi sliced

100 grams oatcakes (blitzed into crumbs)

a little butter

A small bunch parsley chopped

RECIPE.

Fry the onion, spring onion and garlic in some rapeseed oil, season, add lemon juice, parsley and the stock and mix well.

Meanwhile preheat the oven to 180 degrees.

Place the courgettes and sweet potato in an oven proof dish, season and drizzle some oil, take the onion mix off the heat place on top of the courgettes and sweet potato and transfer to the oven for about fifteen minutes.

When cooked take out the oven and place the halloumi on the mixture, transfer back to oven and leave in for twenty minutes. Meanwhile heat some butter in a frying pan and add the blitzed oat cakes so they are coated. Leave to one side.

Remove the dish from the oven and place the oatcake mix on top and place back in oven one last time. Cook for a further fifteen minutes. Remove and enjoy!

v e g g i e s

WARM BROAD BEAN & HALLOUMI SALAD

2 SERVINGS

· ·

 15"   BALANCE   VEGGIES

· ·

INGREDIENTS.
· · · · · · · · · · · ·

250 grams cooked broad beans

250 grams halloumi cheese cubed

1 small onion chopped

50 grams baby spinach

70 grams chestnut mushrooms sliced

1 tbsp rape seed oil

Squeeze half lemon

Seasoning

1 small chilli deseeded & chopped

RECIPE.
· · · · · · · · ·

Heat the oil in a pan, fry the onion and chilli for couple minutes.

Add the halloumi until it has browned a little, then add the broad beans and the mushrooms.

Let them cook for few minutes, add lemon juice and season.

Wilt the spinach into the pan, stir well and serve.

Eat on its own or with chicken or fish.

v e g g i e s

FALAFEL

2 SERVINGS

 45" BALANCE VEGGIES

INGREDIENTS.

15 grams fresh coriander

400 grams tinned chick peas (drained)

2 or 3 oat cakes

1 tbsp rape seed oil

splash water

RECIPE.

Preheat the oven until 160 degrees. Have a baking sheet ready.

Place the chick peas and coriander into a food processor, blitz for thirty seconds and then add some water, the oil and the oatcakes.

Blitz again until the consistency has thickened.

Roll into balls and place on baking sheet and bake in oven for 30 minutes or until cooked through and slightly crispy on outside.

MUSHROOM, PROSCIUTTO & SUNDRIED TOMATO BREGG

2 SERVINGS

 15"   BALANCE   VEGGIES

INGREDIENTS.

150 grams ground almonds

120 grams chopped cooked mushrooms

1 tbsp baking powder

1 tbsp stock

Four slices prosciutto crudo

1 egg

splash water

seasoning

Four sun dried tomatoes chopped

RECIPE.

Preheat oven to 160 degrees, meanwhile line a loaf tin with parchment paper.

In large bowl add the almonds, baking powder, stock and seasoning. Stir well and add the water and mix again.

Add the egg and mix as it will become quite sticky. Add all the other ingredients.

Season again and mix until all combined together. Transfer to the loaf tin and place in oven.

Cook for forty minutes. When cooked it will come clean when a knife is placed in.

Serve with salad and lots of butter!

MUSHROOM & GARLIC PATE

2 SERVINGS

 15" BALANCE VEGGIES

INGREDIENTS.

120 grams chestnut mushrooms roughly chopped

30 grams butter

2 cloves garlic

70 grams creme fraiche

Seasoning

RECIPE.

Fry the mushrooms and garlic in the butter, season well and when ready transfer to a food processor.

Whizz until mixed well and add the creme fraiche and whizz again.

Transfer to a container and place in the fridge for couple hours before eating to set.

BEAN, SWEET POTATO AND MUSHROOM CASSOULET

2 SERVINGS

 15"   BALANCE   VEGGIES

INGREDIENTS.

2 medium sweet potatoes; peeled, diced

1 small onion sliced

2 spring onions, sliced

3 cloves garlic, peeled, chopped

1 yellow pepper, diced

1 tin flageolet beans (265grams)

3 to 4 large chestnuts mushrooms, sliced

1 heaped tsp Buillion stock

Seasoning

70 cl non alcoholic ale

RECIPE.

Heat some butter in a pan and fry the onions, spring onions and garlic, after they are browned add the sweet potato, season well and add the stock and the ale.

Leave for about ten minutes to cook and add the mushrooms, peppers, kale and beans. Leave to cook for about twenty minutes.

Season again and leave to cook on very slow heat for about ten minutes.

Serve with rocket and tahini.

HALLOUMI SALAD WITH TAHINI DRESSING

2 S E R V I N G S

 15"   BALANCE   VEGGIES

INGREDIENTS.

20 grams rocket or lambs lettuce

Handful cherry tomatoes, chopped

Half c ourgette, spir alised

Rape seed oil for frying

3 slices halloumi

For the dressing

1 tbsp tahini

tbsp oil oil

1 tbsp cider vinegar

Seasoning

RECIPE.

In a frying pan heat up the oil and fry the courgette, meanwhile place the rocket and the tomatoes in a dish.

Slice the halloumi read for frying. When the courgette is cooked place onto the rocket an add the halloumi to the pan.

Fry on each side until golden brown. Make the dressing and season well. Add the halloumi to the salad and drizzle the dressing on top.

Yum!

veggies

SPLIT PEA, PECORINO & PARLSEY FRITTATA

2 SERVINGS

 15"   BALANCE   VEGGIES

INGREDIENTS.

100 grams cooked and soaked split peas

50 grams chopped pecorino

Small bunch chopped parsley

Half r ed onion chopped

2 cloves garlic

1 tsp chilli flakes

2 beaten eggs

Seasoning

RECIPE.

Heat a non stick pan using a little butter.

Cook the onion, garlic and chilli flakes and after about five minutes add the split peas, mix well and season well.

Then add the cheese, parsley and when they have been cooking for about five minutes more, arrange them so they are in the middle of the pan and then pour in the beaten egg.

Use a pallet knife when the edge of the egg begins to cook and run it round so it can't stick.

When cooked on one side flip it over. When cooked then serve with a salad.

Yum!

proteins

· · · · · · · · · · · · · · · · · · · ·

CHICKEN & MUSHROOM QUINOTTO WITH GREENS

4 SERVINGS

 45" NUTS

INGREDIENTS.

150 grams quinoa (cooked)

2 cooked chicken legs (bones removed)

1 red onion chopped

2 cloves garlic

2 small yellow peppers chopped

3 large chestnut mushrooms sliced

1 cup chicken stock

1 tsp Bouillon stock

seasoning

2 large cabbage leaves sliced

Bunch fresh mint chopped

RECIPE.

Fry some butter in a pan and add the onion and garlic, cooked down and add the peppers, season and the cooked quinoa.

Add the Bouillon, the mushrooms and cook for about fifteen minutes. Stir well.

Add the chicken stock, let it reduce for further ten minutes and add the chicken.

Taste and season more if needed. Leave to cook and add the cabbage so it wilts.

Serve with the chopped mint and enjoy!

treats

ENERGY BALLS

4 SERVING • DOUBLE INGREDIENTS

 45" NUTS FRUITS

INGREDIENTS.

100 grams dark chocolate (85%) but you can use what you like

130 grams medjool dates

100 grams cashew nuts

3 tbsp rice syrup

RECIPE.

Place the nuts and choc in a food processor and blitz, add the dates and blitz until all mixed.

Put the processor on slow and through the top pour in the rice syrup.

Until it has all been blinded together.

Roll into balls and place on parchment paper and refrigerate for couple hours before eating.

Yum!

ALMOND AND DATE CAKE

4 SERVING • DOUBLE INGREDIENTS

 60" ALMOND MILK NUTS

 FRUITS OVEN 140°C

INGREDIENTS.

3 x tbsp rapeseed oil

2 x tbsp rice syrup

3 eggs

1 tsp cinnamon

4 medjool dates chopped up

150 grams ground almonds

3 tbsp chopped nuts (any type)

2 tbsp almond milk

1 tbsp baking powder

RECIPE.

Preheat the oven to 140 degrees or gas mark 4.

Line a spring back tin with parchment paper.

Take a large bowl and add the oil and syrup.

Mix well and then add the eggs one by one. Add the ground almonds and the baking powder and mix well then add the cinnamon.

Mix again before adding the nuts and dates and milk. Mix well and place in the tin and bake in the oven for about 45 minutes.

Place a knife in and if it comes out smooth it is cooked. Leave to cool.

CUSTARD TARTS

4 SERVING • DOUBLE INGREDIENTS

 45" NUTS OVEN  160°C

INGREDIENTS.

For the pastry;

150 grams ground almonds

2 tbsp grape seed oil

1 egg

For the custard;

2 cups almond milk

3 eggs

3 heaped tbsp coconut sugar

1tsp vanilla extract

RECIPE.

Preheat the oven to 160 degrees, have a muffin tin ready, this will make about ten tarts.

Place the ground almonds in a large bowl and add the oil, and mix well.

Add the egg and mix well, bind together with your hand. If made in advance then wrap and leave in fridge for an hour.

Roll out and cut into circles with a cookie cutter and add to muffin tins and place in oven.

Cook for about twenty minutes.

Add all the ingredients to a large bowl and whisk until well blended. Leave to chill for half hour.

When pastry cases are cooked remove from oven and ladle some custard into each tart case and place back in oven at 160 degrees for a further thirty minutes.

When rready emove leave to cool and enjoy with tea.

CHOCOCONUT

4 SERVING • DOUBLE INGREDIENTS

 60" FRUITS

INGREDIENTS.

100 grams desiccated coconut

2 tbsp coconut oil

20 grams block coconut cream

2 tbsp rice malt syrup

80 grams dark choc

RECIPE.

Melt the coconut oil in a pan, then add the cream and melt this too.

Add the coconut and coat it with the melted oil and cream.

Add the syrup and stir well.

Line a small dish with parchment paper and spoon the coconut mixture in it.

Leave in the fridge to set for about 2 hours.

When set, melt the chocolate and spoon over the set coconut and place in fridge once again for about an hour.

Chop into squares and serve! Much better than the commercial stuff!

desserts

NECTARINE & ROSE WATER CRUMBLE WITH ALMONDS & PISTACHIOS

4 SERVING • DOUBLE INGREDIENTS

 45" NUTS FRUITS OVEN 160°C

INGREDIENTS.

4 nectarines chopped into medium pieces

2 tbsp rose water

50 grams of almonds and pistachio (blitzed)

1 tbsp rice malt syrup

RECIPE.

Cook the nectarines with the rose water in a pan for ten minutes. Blitz the nuts and leave to one side.

Preheat the oven to 160 degrees meanwhile. When the nectarines have cooked then place them in a dish and place the nuts on the top, spoon over the rice syrup and place in oven for about 15 to 20 minutes.

Serve with yoghurt. Yum!!!

v e g g i e s

PINEAPPLE CRUMBLE

2 SERVINGS

 15"   BALANCE   VEGGIES

INGREDIENTS.

half pineapple cut into chunks

1 tbsp rice syrup

1 tbsp butter

For the crumble

60 grams oats

1 tbsp butter

RECIPE.

Preheat the oven to 160 degrees. Place the pineapple in a heat proof dish, and pour over the syrup, and place the butter strategically over the pineapple. Place in the oven for about twenty minutes. Meanwhile in a pan, heat the butter and add the oats once it has all melted. Take off the heat and coat the oats in the melted butter. Leave to one side, and when the pineapple has cooked take out the oven and place the oats over the fruit. Put back in oven and cook for another fifteen minutes. When cooked serve with creme fraiche. Yum!

Printed in the United States
By Bookmasters